PAGAN TO THE CORE

Pagan to the Core

Máighréad Medbh

ARLEN HOUSE

PAGAN TO THE CORE

is published in 2014 by
ARLEN HOUSE
42 Grange Abbey Road
Baldoyle
Dublin 13
Ireland
Phone/Fax: 353 86 8207617
Email: arlenhouse@gmail.com

Distributed internationally by
SYRACUSE UNIVERSITY PRESS
621 Skytop Road, Suite 110
Syracuse, NY 13244–5290
Phone: 315–443–5534/Fax: 315–443–5545
Email: supress@syr.edu

ISBN 978–1–85132–088–2, paperback

Typesetting: Arlen House

Publisher Note
Pagan to the Core incorporates *The Making of a Pagan*, first published in 1990 by Blackstaff Press, Belfast

CONTENTS

INTRODUCTION

Máighréad Medbh

I wrote *The Making of a Pagan* in 1988 and 1989, around the time when I first realised that my emotional experiences had a socio-political context. As a result, the sequence exhibits all the anger of a political ingénue, but primarily I wanted to write a series of impressions of my life, and there was also inherent rage at the various annoyances that the flesh itself arouses. 'Where does the anger come from?' a journalist asked me at the time. It was a good question, but I sidestepped it and retorted, 'Where does it go to?'

Why do people let the indignation go? Because they learn to cope? Or they were peaceful enough to begin with? Maybe they fear the exposure anger brings, the necessity to act? I was afraid, and *The Making of a Pagan* is an attempt to push past the fear.

Looking at some of the reviews again, I found that whatever was brash or scatological got the most attention. Understandably, I suppose, but no-one mentioned 'Beat' or 'Mother Shades', two of my favourites, as they are what they express. There was sometimes an assumption that I intended to shock. I didn't. I intended to be honest and direct. I was trying to expose myself, so I was immersed in what I hoped would be the organic representation of each chosen moment and thought.

Maybe I did know that some people would disapprove, because it was a struggle to use words like 'cunt', 'fart' and 'fuck'. I rarely said those words myself, but I felt they were in me and it was true to say them. It was much later that I realised my performances had created a stir. There was a sermon in the church in my home town, and an appearance on RTÉ brought letters of complaint. Those responses had a nil value for me, though I was glad I hadn't courted approval.

The Disaffected Country Girl and A Minor Metropolis, the new sequence in this edition, arose from a commission by Liam Carson in 2010 to write poems about Dublin for the *Imram* festival. *The Making of a Pagan* was far from my mind, unconsulted, when I started to explore my experience of the city in the best way I could – by tracing the road there from 'picturesque' Newcastle West. I found my self splitting, looking at 'her', the character in me who was the growing girl, and 'you', the adult character whose actions I struggle to direct and understand. Same essential subject matter, different view.

I've made a few changes to the original text. Punctuation has been revised in places and more effective phrasing used where I thought necessary. But the bulk of the content is the same and stanza organization generally as it was when first published by Blackstaff Press in Belfast in that different, but in a way still present, time.

– Dublin, 2013

The Making of a Pagan

A New Place

Like a forgotten nut
it broke
one night.
Crack.
I never had the knack
of walking by a chasm.
In I went and down.
First there was a juicy feel,
white pulpish feel.
Nothing like the smell of white
in a strange nut.
I made a bed there,
just under the shell.
Squalch.
It was nice then,
the shell pressing on the
juicy white pulp pressing on me.
Better than a downy bed
down down in the country.
Squalchy in dreams
I bounced, spluttered,
swept on,
slushed in gullies.
Dark I went and grey
through a ploughed tunnel.
But then I opened all my eyes.
A new place.

Womb

The return journey is
the only journey there is;
from light and teeming space
in search of the dark place,
back.
But there is colour here,
treasures hung high on the walls,
a cave that would be black
but they and the hint of a door
prism it.
I pick up the thread that led me back.
It pulls taut.
Down it in royal welcome
the treasures pulley towards me –
a blue satin bed-jacket
a peach dress
a white cardboard box shaking with spools
a yellow tin box (flower-embossed).
How it was.

MOTHER

Clack go her glasses
down on her nose.
Raatum go her false teeth.
Suck suck suck on the thread
to thread a needle
to turn a hem
to shorten a dress for me.

Swallow say eyes
in a goldfish bowl.
National Health doesn't care.
They brace me up
deface me
open me
white my hair.

Her Lap

Her lap is a country
where promises hang open.
Across the long chasm her magic apron
makes a bridge smelling
of baked bread and tarts,
vouches safe.

I want to hammock you,
shrink myself back baby-size,
listen close to the sway
of your full green tree.

Her lap is the place of all home,
where everything fruits and dies.

Can I play upon your notes like before,
bounce happy on your knee
to the beat of your
one-tight, two-loose flesh?
Look, I can sing the tune –
Die diddle diddle die …

I have become monster
in my own shadow,
pressing on your land like this.

A Peach Dress

blue and white day
and a peach dress
oh and a cuddly black
smooth black and brown and white dog
and a white cat
and his one blue eye
and his one green eye
and waking up to the
purr purr purr
of blackie
deep among the sheets

bok clack whirr
against the wall
i am billy jean king
i know them all
white dresses and all
dresses i cut them from paper
and hang them on dolls
white with golden stars
midnight blue pale pink
and a lime green

i will marry in lime green
like a wild nymph
fresh from the fields
still damp
i will marry my only only
i will dance for you daddy
one two three and a
one two three and a
ballet bounce and a twirl
and a purr purr
pirouette

A Scape of Country

In all the gathered globe
never was a country like this.
This is green below red
below yellow below white
below blue.

Down the boreen
hedges hoard clusters of lush.
Places for fairies to sleep,
fairies tiny as pin tips.

Tonight the moon will rise
like a piece of furze
flying from a hill fire.
It will turn the sky
highwayman blue.

The Swing

This is the best world.
The swing creaks back and toward.
I pretend piranha underneath raise heads,
but I raise feet and stretch them out.

The sun makes pictures of gooseberry bushes.
Scents come dizzy up for air,
spread a veil on shone hair.
I should wear a parasol.

I pick blackcurrants in my slip,
squeeze none too tight.
Sugar plantations must be like.
Or naked grapes
in honeyed purple
French extremes.

SARDINES

our house is divided
one part for him
one for all of us
we're like these sardines
i'm twisting their key
to let them out
to let me in
like he twists her key
and she moves like he says
and she stays in at night
like i'd like to twist
a knife in his gut
especially on fridays
with one tin for him
and one for all of us

THE HALL

There is a long hall
where I and my brother wrestle.
I in my vest and navy knickers,
he in white shorts.
I am a brave and keep-out-the-towel warrior,
but this is love.

He teaches me the world.
When alone, I make a street.
Shops with skimped bikinis
thrown in windows.
Soft somethings for high-gloss girls.

A long altar
where I marry my toys.
Teddies with dolls
in christening robes.
Ave Maria to you –
Queen of the May-be-someday
but anyhow a joy.

When day disperses
the hall has reflected light only.
Father's call flies down it.
There is a rosary
waiting to be strung out.
Then, at least, to bed.

Taste

Legs are pins
stuck in cushions.
Softer, warm.
A ruler slid between them
has a hot smell after.

Three fingers, like monkeys,
are climbing to the top,
where great leaves fold
into a mushroom cap.

What gills I have.
Twiddle. Jiggle.
That starts a fruity feel.
Sniff, and sweet as apple tart.

My stomach has a knot.
What for?
Flake out the white –
mmm, need lots of sugar.

Or will you try
my own ear's honey?
Straight out tangy,
the taste of me.

SOLDIER

How does he dare
to look in my direction?
How does he think to put me down?
I am soldier, just like he was.
Stand back.
Left right, left right.
How the foot is shoulder high.
He will not stare!

I can be secret agent,
bag over the shoulder
like in the comic,
gun at hand.
I bob down by low walls,
shadow ash trees.
I see you.
You don't.
I listen at doors.
Nothing good.

Blast into stone houses.
Look I have dynamite
sizzling red at the tip.
I will slap it in his face
and run
and not regret.
Or hand grenade his hairy thighs.
Or die for his poison.
Or
Fucking Bastard
burn his eyes.

A Flow of Blood

The dog sniffs up my leg.
I know what he smells.
Blood under my dress.
Will he tell?
The fishy smell.
The must-be-washed.
Clean my nakedness.
Tidy my mess.

I was waiting for this.
My secret importance.
Will it soak my pants,
drip onto the ground,
        onto the tiles in church?
Will everyone know?

First among my friends –
I have become woman.
I suffer like saints.
My clothes held close,
I walk with care.
Delicate.
Wise.
Blessed.
Virgin.

Man

'What a piece of work …'

The abiding colossus
has one foot in my bedroom,
one where I play and read;
a hand where I cook,
a hand where I sit to eat.
He sticks his head
through the roof of my house
and sings, perennial.
He nods when I move, saying,
'Take me with you when you stay'.

I learn the female is a clam to be forced
and she must never learn how.
The soft are the only worth considering –
those who feed, wash socks,
listen to rambling wisdoms over pints,
plumb the unspoken.
Men know how the world can be pushed around.

Men make time tick.
We wait for them,
wane before clanged armour
and bounded white.
We turn them princes.
They cannot do without –
especially us pale pink,
no-make-up, leafy
country girls.

Women make and mend,
ourselves also,
draw in our brains for fear of spill.

We are buttons on their best soutanes,
hang, cruxes, from their necks,
wreathe about their middles.

They carry huge loads
to the furthest army of great houses,
climb, ass-burdened,
to steep thrones.
When they tire, troubled,
we sit and kiss.

We seep out in weeping rivers,
but they love-stroke us,
spark up the female fire,
move close like stalkers,
finally open us with a silent push.
We lie and lie before they come,
their tokens, tributes,
running at our skirts.

Turning Sixteen

Always cycling.
Always wearing odd clothes
sent from America or passed down.
Summer dresses make the best wear.
In winter I have one good coat
and one for hacking.

The town girls have the latest –
faded jeans, jazzy tops.
They smoke too, on the hill to school.
I'm better than that.
I smoke in my private room.

I must have the biggest bottom ever,
flopping like unmoulded jelly.
My face is a tomato
when I'm asked to speak.
My hair is always tossed.

There must be a secret.
Are they never cold,
must wear caps and flatten their hair?
How are their legs so brown?

How can I be a film star,
with my scar
and my yellow teeth
and my phlegmy throat?

The Boreen

From the inside of town when the library's closed,
it's a good cycle home through the night.
I'm all in my head with a girly dream
of boys and cars and primrosed fields
where lovers chase and fall and kiss
and wedding rings and beds.
The millionaire's window has no blind;
you can see the designer stove,
and the couple standing sometimes
at the slanted, tinted glass.
Across the road, no curtains drawn, the living-room
of Brady's own-built bungalow is all on show.
They don't mind we see them living, children dancing,
adults idling, moving toys, visitors arriving.
I can't imagine life without a closed front door,
a curtained night and secrets in the room.

I veer the bike and turn towards home.
The boreen is total pitch.
My front-lamp is a spear of light
that pierces out a path.
The leaves remind me of the dress
a queen of England wore.
My wheels are dancing minuets
across a whispered floor.

But what?

My hands tighten on the handlebars
Swerve
Bright stones?
Eyes black and white
In the middle of the
Man's standing body

Staring
Says hello
Can he stop me?
Keep pushing
Pedal Pedal
He's speaking
Wait come 'ere a minute
I think he's that O'Brien from the well
Pedal Pedal
Girls not safe
Mammy told me
Just last Friday Margie
He pulled her knickers down
I must escape
My chest will spill out
The pounding pounding
Throat is blocked
I'm getting there
Away away
The light of home
I'm there
The gate sings shut behind
I'm at the door

He's home.
Compose.

First Love

The plumb-stomached summer of it
leaves me abstract,
piking vacant halves on hay cocks,
staring vastly down the field
to stamp his face on every frond and shoot.

Last night the dance,
a whirl-candy, pink-floss time,
girl-massed, boy-crushed.
'Can I have this one?'
Or a hand poking,
a rude beck.
'Why not?'

Then him.
His head turrets the host,
black on dull.
I'm here.
Feel the rush-winding
of my sum and substance out to you.
He sees. His broad, farming face grins.
The skyward eyes.

He bows his head when we dance,
hangs his lips on my neck.
My closed lids make a cell of each move,
the legs brushed,
the hand angling up from the waist.
He can feel,
he can feel through my blouse.
He is all about me,
huge as darkness.

and then
locked on the stairs
the first
the soft spoonful palping
down tongue
clipped to the lifelong suck
curl slouch about the teeth
setting the inside lip dancing
like a harem
held to the last delicious
strangle just above the heart

my own
the only ever
marry marry marry
white and gold
white and gold
his slow walk
his huge hands
his tongue on my neck
                    in my mouth

The new blue dress next Sunday
and hair combed back from the ears.
He kisses my ears.
I have scrubbed this cup forty times,
soaked in suds,
the way he bubbled me up,
blew me into full, light air,
opened the window and
Puff

Mother Shades

down where
the shades are
i pray her
not fade
into
days now
she hardly hears
the needs
i speak
a step toward
is
a step in wake
of a weird wind
i pray her
not rescind
her helping smile
her sounding look
that now seem
lookaway

Beat

white steps
white day
steel white mountain

jump stair to see
her jump stair to see
her jump stair to see

standing at the tip top
pale-eyed speaker of
the end of the low bend
she has been taken

no she is not
away no she is not
away no she is not

come black hole in ashen day
skirl scrape suck away all that
colours flowers stands
and lift me high
to heaviside
to bolt and thunder
spark and geyser
sweat and swelter
wave and ray

galloping drumbeat
hip hop tumble
how many pulses
all in the body
leg thrum hand thrum
eye in a vibrate

vamp in the fleshpack
where can I fly

fly to home where
she is less a beating
face a vision
cannot kiss a face that's brazen
she's abating

she is meat
she is deadbeat
she is deadbeat
she is beaten
dead she is beaten
dead she is beaten
she is beat
she is dead

First Night in Dublin

There's a girl in the jacks boxed to the wall. She's in her scrimped-for jumper and jeans, all brand-city-new. But god, does she look like she's rupturing inside. Even her knees are crying. She can't stand up, she's so brittle. Partly the drink, I suppose, but mostly she was getting cross-brained out there. The talk was just bosses' habits, jokes she couldn't understand (What's so funny about 'coming'?), half-made comments with a sly nod or a rat-tat-tat laugh. What was that he said? What's dope? What did he mean, 'Balls to you'? How can he talk like that? Balls are a man's test ... But that other man looked nice, sounded intellectual too. He hadn't noticed her, or maybe he had. Yeah, he'd smiled. Maybe he thought she was pretty and demure, not like the rest of them. The things they said! But she knows, she knows ... nothing, blast it. She's never even heard of *The Smiths*. Why can't they talk about sincere things – themselves, what they truly feel? Politics even. She knows about politics. She's great on theories. That Englishman she met in the parish hall at home thought she was the most interesting girl around, even though he was 34 and she was only 17. So did Brian. That's what he liked about her, he said. But it wasn't enough, was it? He said she should let herself go more, dance without self-consciousness, shake her hips. 'Don't be so stiff', he said, and then he barely kissed her. Awake all night, lying on the bed, and he only touched her breast once, saying after a minute of awkward stroking, 'If you want to call a halt ...' Call a halt, oh god, he's the one boy, the only, she'd nearly make love to. Oh and it's all such a starless time. She was a stranger to everyone at home, and now she's stranger still.

So she's scrunched up, a sodden primrose, damped by the evening and battered by lovers' feet. She knows she must leave this box – some rude person just said, 'Hey, what are you doing in there, playing with yourself?' – so she dries up, hauls her body, conjures her best I–am-perfectly-in-control-and-who-are-you look, and slowly faces out.

On Calls

At eighteen it's hard to be a law-enforcer.
I must knock on doors, enter and question.

At eighteen I'm in the balloon of idealism.
I study humans through the microscope of myself.

They call me a guardian of the fund.
Picture me in armour and spear.

I'm rehearsed in de-focus.
Every time I knock on a door
I imagine myself elsewhere.

FILE: Imelda Makum. Report of death received. Pension book cashed for four months after date of death. By whom? Recover debt.

A thin woman answers.
'No, I'm no relation. She lived alone in her flat'.
What next? I have an oblique mind. Oh, a niece?
Where? Excellent. Thank you and goodbye.
I reach the house, a weighted feather.
'The Pension book? Yes, I cashed it. Wasn't I entitled?
She was a crotchety old bitch. No matter what I did,
she complained. She was bedridden for the past year,
wouldn't go into hospital. Mother of Divine Jesus, I
deserve to be canonised after her. I washed her, fed
her, cleaned up her slops. Running from here to there,
she ringing me up in the small hours for nothing. My
life is ruined over her'.
This I can't help. I stare at the file.
You'll have to pay it back, I'm afraid. No way out.
'But I got no allowance for looking after her'.
Sorry, you should have claimed one.

Outside, the day is still fresh – blue and white as the virgin. I'm in a daydream. Will he phone? Please let him phone. The way he kissed my neck. I dream him the father of my children. Now, Sharon, listen to your Daddy.

FILE: Mary Anne Brady. Unmarried mother. Review this case re change of address.

She's not expecting me. A man opens the door. Two other men are sitting in the only apart-from-the-bed-room. The child runs dirty, half-dressed, in circles. I've not studied the file. My god, she shares my birthday and she looks like an old woman. Eighteen in a balloon.

We sit in the kitchenette.

Any contact with the father?

'No, I don't know where he is. He ran off when he found out I was expecting'.

I'm conscious of the three men in the not-the-bed-room. Brothers, I suppose. I hope. There are too many to be of significance. They could be friends. Some men and women are friends, they really are. I should ask. I leaf through the pages, playing for time.

'They're my brothers in the other room'.

Relief.

Claimant's brothers, I write, were present on the occasion of my visit. No sign of co-habitation. I'm damned if I'm going to search her wardrobe and under the bed.

Sky again. Almost time for lunch and a read of the paper. I must read that article on the Japanese social system. I must write him a love letter.

On the River

Summer on the Shannon,
where it's always holidays.
Boat to boat,
bow to stern.
We are girls alone.

We moor the craft
and go down to the pub,
where the hard-muscled men
from the power station
wear white shirts and denims,
medallions to show off broad chests.
They eye us, sweet-as-pie us.
The one I get is strong,
talks like a gentleman, sings.
I sing.
We drink and the crowd sways
and oh the world is merry.
He kisses me on the German's boat.
I note the knicker-navy sky
and throw up over the side.

Back on our own rocking craft
the rain is flooding the fo'c'sle,
while Mary snores in the other cabin.
I'm in my clothes on the top bunk,
he in my clothes on top of me.
Men always kiss and feel
and I don't fully understand
what's next.
It seems I'm *Operation Body*.
My hand feels something fleshy and long.
That's the part I want to forget.
They don't really have one

that sticks right up and into you.
The water sweeps against the sides.
I'm surrounded.
'I don't want to have sex or anything'.
My demurral drowns in the rising tide.
What is that pain?
I think my scream will send
the birds calling,
bring a rescue mission,
but no, the water holds its rhythm,
drums like mania,
and this open throttle sinks in the maelstrom.

Summer on the river, raining.

Coming Out

my hands began it
and now I love it
my cunt is swelling
thinking of it
thinking of a tongue on it

a warm ache between my legs
my hands begin
stroke up my breasts
my breasts are steaming
nipples standing staring
my hands are drawing the world
from the mound of my head
to the round of my small toe
feel my legs
the inside thigh beginning to blush
then shining
then my stomach a mass of tingle
I touch my clit it sings
a touch is a step inside
I am queen and land
where east meets west
my hands unclose a passage
north to south
my face is full upon me
all of me my face
all become a globe
the width of my spread legs
and between them
the centre is thickening
the lips are pursing out
I am speeding up
my hands are driving
my cunt is driving

I am zooming to my inner space
only one direction
I am in there
it's blowing out
ballooning out
my self steering
my self steered
all a flow
all a rush
a tidal wave
wet on my fingers
heat rivers in my thighs
in my tail
my tail is spinning shaking swishing
I am the world
I am spinning
taking space
making whirlwinds out of space
I am space
I am spilling in
I am spilling out
I am coming
streaming steaming
coming coming coming coming
coming coming coming coming
out

PMT

the weaTHeR iS swePT doWN
iT iS a puRPLe floWeR
peTaLS goiNG puTPuT
aT mY cheeKS aND haiR
iT iS wouND iN a rouGH sheeT

peoPLe beaR iN
buLGiNG buLLS eYeS
taLK tuRNS faCToRY wheeLs
                faCToRY wheeLS
claRRioN caRRioN caLL
iNSiDe mY nuT a kiNDLiNG thRoB

i haVe doNe wroNG aGaiN
leT sliP the waY i aM
leT free the rouGH woRD
aND theY staReD
no theY wouLD noT haVe saiD
theY aRe kiND
noT i

i waNT to shooT
spLiT the breasTBoNe
suLLY the iNNoCeNT
proBe the cuNT oF
a siXTY-yeaR-oLD viRGiN
taKe a prieST'S priCK
beTWeeN mY liPS

giVe me a staTue
aND i'LL shaTTeR
aND theN mYSeLF

aND theN ruN heaDLeSS
oVeR a briDGe-eND

i aM woRTH a peBBLe
i aM woRTHY oF no looKS
                    no proFeRReD haND
keeP youR faKe giFTS
i knoW wheRe youR haTe lieS
you waNT mY cuNT oN a diSH
youR teeTH aRe baRe
beHiND youR smiLe

you wouLD woLF me
iF you couLD caTCH aND cooK me
buT i wieLD cleaVeR fiRST
aND buRST mYSeLF

hoW maNY skiNS haS a
suPeR suPeR-eGo

giVe uS a kniFe
giVe uS a scaLPeL
giVe uS a boDY
oN a screaMiNG beD

yeS i wiLL toRTuRe
oNe mY eYeS
two buRN skiN to ciGaReTTe steaKS
tiLL i aM raW raW reD
cuT oFF mY fooT
thRee riGHT
fouR leFT
duMP boDY
iN faST ruNNiNG waTeR

Crawling

I never knew so much could breed
from so little fornication.
My knickers are crawling
with green things and orange things,
the murmur and thrust of a nation.

Long heads, long legs,
see-through bodies eating at me.
There they are laughing,
leg on knee, saying,
'Hee hee –
we spawned without sound
in the forest of G,
we grew with the force of secrecy.
You won't kill us now with soap and a towel.
We'll make you squirm for your ecstasy'.

I slept with two within two weeks,
one silly, one insane.
I think it was the silly one
who drove me up a lane
and told me how he'd love to
with me then, and then again.
And then he did and did again.
I know he didn't mean
to sow the seed of foreigners
among my home-grown fields.

Now, even though I smile and smile,
those villains bite and seethe.
I can't reach down to scratch at them
while you're around to see.
I've got some cream to burn them out
before they burn me down;

then back to sweet and wild romance.
It's just love's bitter crown!

ENGAGEMENT

If it weren't for that
honey-haloed,
white-lighted,
beam-through-fresh-open-blinds
look of yours,
I would never have made your fable,
your Aeneas and Naoise
glued in my own blue package.

If it weren't for their
hens' cluck –
'Oh he's lovely,
a sound man,
keeps you quiet' –
their shoving of rings,
their man-sized praise,
I would not have worn you.

If it were only
your laughs,
your deep down
oh-so-traditional honour,
your sporting maleness,
your permanent and prisoning job,
I could have strolled, full-directed,
to the other side of the world.

Nights With Anne

nights with anne
and the headlights are on
and the alcohol current
is rushing my head upriver
i'll escape this present
i'll fly to the moon and back

she has the brightest
pair of eyes so prophetic
that ever spoke spear
to my own dark horse

steal a saddle to another world
we are high-ho-thunder away
we are saved
from the wolfing plastics
        the tin buttresses
        the right attitudes
        the feminine assent

strike a song there
for i and i am
in sudden ignition
my own bright key
my own fused force
propelled by me
not men not god
but the female whirl
is fuel to our moves
as we sing
raise cries
raise glasses
raise skirts
to the knee

to the waist
to the neck
to the head
to the
come on up baby
I'm home

The Greenhouse Effect

I care about the greenhouse effect. I really do. But it'd be great to combine ecology with a bit of excitement. I always go for the powerful ones, so I'm concentrating on the speaker. He's composed and confident, talks like we were all sitting in his house. I like his pale blue eyes. Oh, I could sing him that song. *Linger on, your pale blue eyes*. There's no other girl in the room he'd think about, I reckon. The two attractive ones are with men. I could have him all right. Oh, but he's probably married. No ring, but that doesn't mean anything. Maybe he's doing it the ecological way, shacking up with a torrid, hippy beauty who makes clay ornaments, knits and sews all their clothes, does gigantic tapestries and has their kitchen full of herbs and spices. He wouldn't have much time for my baked beans and sausages.

He has a slight beer belly. Surely ecologists don't drink, not to excess anyway? It's a beautiful world all right, when I look at it. Of course, O'Connell Street is a far cry from the Amazon. It's hard to picture all those trees, miles upon miles of them. God, I'd love to see Brazil. What was that he said, 'wife'? No, something about 'life'. I wouldn't mind living in West Cork among the natives; no need for electricity or anything. I'd feel like a god. He does. He doesn't look like he was born in the countryside. The faraway hills that used to be green, I suppose. Let's hie to the hee-lands.

He certainly seems to know his stuff. He's quoting figures now. 0.6% increase in temperature in the last hundred years. Was that a one foot rise in sea level?
'My god, my melons', says one woman.
If the city centre gets flooded, that's me upskuttled,

not to mention all the poor people in the flats. Come to think of it, no-one *has* mentioned them.
'Of course', says the curly-headed one, 'if people had to move from the city centre, it would affect us in the mountains'.
A sore place to be affected.
Now to the important bit. What to do about it? Good question there from a Northern woman. They always get to the point.
'Lobby', he says. 'Lobby your politicians. If everybody in this room called their local politician tomorrow, you'd be surprised at the difference it would make'.
I certainly would. Most of the people here haven't a clue what's going on or what to ask a politician to do – myself included.
'Don't spend money', he counsels. 'The government should bear all the expense of atmosphere-friendly products. The government owes us. That's what we elected them for'.

What government is he talking about? He's English. My god, he actually wants someone else to take the reins, not to mention the responsibility. Some Sir Lancelot he is. I thought he rode to Dublin on a white pony. Turns out he drives a car on leaded petrol, has incandescent bulbs hanging from his ceiling and cuts down trees for firewood. Ecology my foot. Some wild thing he is. There's no excitement here. I'm going home.
Looking at him again, I wouldn't say he'd be great in bed. His hips are the wrong shape. So is his head. Next time I want excitement I'll go to a disco.

F-ING OFF

Finally
I've finished
with your fucks
        your farts
        your filthy sheets
        your faked feelings
        your fluke grins
        your fluthered nights.

I've had it with
our frenzied foutering
in cars and fields
our fined-down fornication.

I'm frying our bond
on a full fire
and then flying free
to a new frontier.

KEEPING THE ANIMAL DOWN

that's the special welcome
eyes brilliant
hands buttered out
a house block-full of fires
heating to the roots of the hair

the wine is opened
dark red and viscous
splutters to the glass's brim
the roast smokes up the nostrils
browns succulently the tongue
that's home

then the blanketed hot-bottled bed
you sink soothed into
until you wish to wake

that's the shock
the first sound is a snort
or a bluster in the throat
next a chair is thrown to the wall
then a knock

familiar now
you remember old tricks
sit silent
lids lowered
while sparking eyes search you

take the apple spiked to your hand
and smile with
all your skin's face
no sudden move when you rise
just a smooth ascent

a quiet push back
from the board

that's the old burning
turning in a vessel kept still
that's keeping the animal down

Original Sin

They tell me my child is a sinner
before he leaves the womb.
Well, he must be a wizard
of a Hallowe'en tricker
if he sins while upside-down
in a bag of water.

They say we made a sinner
because we made a sin
by the evil diction
of the mutual friction
of the basest parts
of our base bodies.

So the woman's body is sin
and the baby lying within
is staring down
at the evil crown
of the demon consort, Quim?

No, says the Catholic priest,
you're having a pagan feast.
The child is a sinner
because of his flesh.
All human beings
are made of trash.
Every heart that beats
and is not baptised
is in Satan's drum,
synchronised.

So what about God,
or is he too big

to jump in the womb
and be infra dig?

DNA is the greatest sin –
Duped by Natural Acumen.
There's my child
with a natural mind
and the churches want to put him
in a moral bind.

But it makes no odds
because my child's a bud
and she'll burst onto earth
like a flower should.
She'll shut up the church
like a Jack-in-the-box
and shout *Up yours*
to the Pope and John Knox.

The Original Witch
will pick up the switch
and turn off the lights
in the steeple's sight.
She will laugh, *Ha Ha,*
She will laugh, *Ho Ho,*
and the walls will go
just like in Jericho.

Baby Skin

My baby,
you cling, I hope,
with resolution
through all these quakes of mine.

I'm riding a demon
when I remember.
My hand slips
to touch the swelling waist that is you
and suddenly I see you,
pale, rounded,
sleeping like you know the world.

I reach your skin and,
teddy close,
you hug me
blind
safe
into tears.

I would live forever to see your face.

Feeding the Baby

– there's a cat on the white line
– my racing car speeds up
– i brake
– the screech fills my head
– fills my head

I open my eyes.
The screech continues.
I had forgotten you in the corner,
your nightly serenade.
Only an hour's break this time
and you grate into my sleep,
turning the key in my back.
I am your pet robot.

I struggle to your cot,
lift your heated ball of a body,
heavier each feed.
Why did I have you?
Your fingers are soft as sausages.
I could bend them backwards.
I could crack your neck
with an even flick.
You have made rivers of my breasts
where you float your smile.
Your chin flops like a drunken thing,
careless in greed.

Now the fiendish colic cries
like ten unstopped alarms.
The trek begins.
I nearly dropped you then
when the heater flex snared my legs.
I almost threw you over my shoulder too.

My back was never so strained.
You're breaking me down.
If you don't stop I'll kill you
and then myself.

You calm to a whimper
and a heavy breathe on my back.
I check in the mirror.
Your eyes, dark and staring,
take in your world.
I look younger than I thought,
our faces an open locket.
Am I mother or child?
Your strange familiarity makes me tremble.
Maybe you'll be a great actor
when you grow.

Song for Aonghus

Who are you that have come in –
a stranger from another race
that have no face but you?
But are they still around you?
You're smiling at the ceiling,
at a room's empty space.

Who are you that have come in,
bringing inspiration home
as your body breathes,
your spirit streams out?
I thought I had lost a life.
I thought the world was a straight line.

Who are you that have come in,
to start me swelling out again
when I had thought me flat?
You're pouring back in
through the lightning chink you made.
Your eyes are not mine,
your hair is not mine,
your sallying smile is all your own;
and still they tell me,
as I am spelled in awe,
that you came from me,
that I had you,
that you are mine.

GERRY

I have come to claim happiness
at your side.
You drew me in somehow
to kiss, I think, what life is,
and look, I am spreading out.
You did it in the dark
and what can I say?
You are straight out special,
catkin beautiful,
lush like green.

There is a dark spot by your side,
where we are both alone, watching.
Do you ever hate me those times –
you in need, I in battle gear,
when it comes to crunches
and I can't say, 'You –
I love you'.

You know the truth.
It's all a cloth I place on me
for fear I'll dust away.
I love your fingers on my hair,
your words a constant flame,
your gentling towards a home,
the pain that spurs hope.
I think a world of women
see the bright blue loving self
that wants to tell me
where's my star
and when my ship is high.
Can I ever lead you in
to fill your own worth out,

to take and eat your own dear soul
and smile your own full mouth?

Nothing for Girls

for Angela

First there's the childsong,
bright blue childsong,
ringing up the air.
You are the sky
and the bird and the cloud
and the scruffy earth
and the mole and the worm
and the world is all people.

Then there's the difference.
Rainbow childsong.
Colours have a place.
You still put faces
on the trees and mushrooms,
but you begin to see borders,
where the sky, where play ends,
school begins.

Borders build a world.
Here's a country for under-twelves.
Here's the teenage nation.
There's the adult set –
they're called 'people'.
Children are sort of apprentice people,
so they don't understand,
so they have all these notions
about things being people
and colours having faces
and sums being boring
and they hate borders.

... and people kind of envy um
although they say they love um

and there's another thing
although they say they love um
they're always trying to change um
more like children love people
because they become like um ...

Children can't understand
why people feel so bitter.
I mean, that's what children aim for –
to be people.
But people are always sorry
they can't be children again.
Because when you're people
you must believe in borders
and don't believe your eyes
or your ears or anything you feel.

There's a little girl
who runs and shouts
and turns cartwheels
and wants to be an artist
and takes on all the boys
and beats them and loves it.
Doesn't see tomboy.
Doesn't see girl-not-boy.
Doesn't see boy-not-girl.
Sees people –
                    in a cartwheel
                    in a colour
                    in a sweat
                    in a treat
people hugging
people crying
people almost split from laughing
people people people ...

There she is
in the comic shop,
looking for herself,
and sees nothing but borders –
what she is not,
what they are,
and suddenly she changes.
'Nothing', she says, head down,
'Nothing for girls'.

Easter 1989

I'm not the woman my great-grandmother was,
to stand on the stairs between her son and the Tans.
'You'll kill me first', she said.

I'm not the woman Bernadette was,
to slap an Englishman's indifferent cheek,
to come back from wounds that would make a corpse.

I'm not the woman Mairéad was,
to yield body and mind
in her people's cause,
that ultimate act.

Always, on the border,
I wish I held the gun,
but time or place has made me small.
I think if they soldiered my streets,
searched me, took my husband out,
I would fight.
But I have seen my father take my mother,
the law take my neighbour,
the church take my womanhood,
and I remain unbloodied.

Where I live, the battle is over.
We work to forget our crazed grandparents
and their mind for a nation
and their nights in ditches
and their songs of defiance.
Every day we retrench,
keep down our heads,
make deeper and wider the dividing line
between us and their hopes,
between us and their guns.

The proud republic they cried
and died for
is a whinging turncoat
picking their pockets
by the side of a new main road,
heading south.

And I am a woman
with children inside me,
bearing out my distance,
taking on my silence,
who will ask where I was
when justice was turned over
and our people murdered,
and whether I sat drinking
in a plush pub,
talking money
while West Belfast bled.

THE FUCKING PONTIFF

The great environmental wound
disturbs his Unholiness, the Godfather,
who stands and counts the trees
that are butchered
and begs in the name of himself
that we build not break.

Under his feet, he crushes
the fine-flowing serpent called woman,
who knows how to make things grow.

His Most Senile Reverence defends
the world's two-thirds blessed poor,
who are far from him
but always with us.
Educate their ignorance.
Eradicate their power.

Under his rule he teaches
to exterminate women in millions
with his brain-bent lessons.

His Grovelling Eminence
kisses the arses of leaders,
but not women. Let them have
children till their arses break
and he'll beatify their broken bones.

Under his body a fiery witch
is stabbed through with his penile sceptre
behind the arras of the tabernacle.

His Dispassionate Majesty
rises to the high chant

of his sterile harem.
His sacred comings butter the bread
they suck and savour.
O, the ecstasy.

Under his throne, the witches are ready
to topple and turn him
            and fuck him
                fuck him
                fuck him

OUR STREETS

These are our streets.
If you are a woman don't look up.
If you do you'll meet the eyes
of idle macho boys.
That's provocation.
If you are a woman and you hear *Hello,*
keep your mouth shut,
your head unturned and cowed.
Huddle up.
Walk faster.
Walk faster.

These are our streets.
If you are a woman and it's night,
wear a long coat and keep
a spray-can to hand,
your only hope.
If you are a woman and you hear a footstep
steadily behind, stay calm,
steal a look,
don't run.
Walk faster.
Walk faster.

At seventy years your sleep is slow.
Kitty feared the night since Martin died,
but most the lonely feel of the single bed
she made downstairs.
One time, the lamp still on,
her *Mills and Boon* lost in her lap,
glasses just above her hanging mouth,
she slept from two to four.
A sudden, fuller darkness woke her,
broke a dream of heaven.

There he was.
Who was?
smell of sweat
tangled hair
eyes of glass
matted coat
murky hands
smell of sweat
staring down
snatched the book
mocking grin
'sexy cunt'
threw her glasses
ripped her nightdress
took a knife and led it down
her sagging body
'rub me mamma
rub me bitch'
smell of sweat
smell of shit
'please don't make me'
like a nightmare
no voice coming
down upon her
smell of shit
tore her open
gashed her bloody
there's no screaming
there's no finish
pierce on push
pierce on darkness
fading out with
pain of piercing
smell of shit
smell of blood

These are our streets.
If you are a woman you see your body
cut up stark at every hand and eye.
Breast here.
Leg there.
If you are a woman you are squared off
in paperback, pasted on the daily news,
on a leash.
Walk faster.
Walk faster.

These are our streets.
If you are a woman you can't drink alone
in pubs where men look
through dark pint glasses,
you're a whore.
If you are a woman and you walk the streets
for money as the ads advise,
you are guiding men astray.
Walk faster.
Walk faster.

In the air-conditioned office,
Sally is a glamour-bird.
Her boss is pleased that she wears *Gucci,*
starts at eight,
is never late for business dates
and always looks like
Cosmopolitan did her up.
Now and then they take the road to Wicklow,
and in a lacy room
they make a certain sort of love,
while his wife shops in London
and her town flat gathers a little dust.
A major merger looming,
off one day to Pittsburgh.

Sally looked a sweet treat,
all the big men said.
'Right', said Roger,
'take my key. She's a tiger.
She'll be expecting me'.

One o'clock.
The door let streak a light
across the floor.
'I'm all satin and champagne,
you old ram'.
Up the light.
three investors
bellies forward
suits of cotton
ties of silk
held her down
smell of smoke
'you can't hurt me
I'll tell Roger'
'cut your whingeing
you're a kitten'
bent her over
smell of smoke
'give her what
she's always wanted'
stripped and saddled
bit and battered
not too badly
left her standing
up and down
in and out
smell of smoke
smell of shit
tore her open
gashed her bloody

there's no screaming
there's no finish
pierce on push
pierce on darkness
fading out with
pain of piercing
smell of smoke
smell of shit

These are our streets.
If you are a woman you must drive
a pram on broken footpaths,
dragging little ones behind,
be always patient.
If you are a woman you must rear
and feed and care and wear well
to be admired.
In tight shoes,
how can you
walk faster?

These are our streets.
If you are a woman you must break the mould,
smash the flashy screen
that makes us meat for pricks
and not for joy.
If you are a woman you must fight
to choose to work, to dress, to fuck,
to look straight in the eye,
to stroll and not
walk faster.

THIRTEEN YEARS DEAD

Thirteen years dead
and she still comes to me.
She says the old things –
'I hate this place but I can't get out'.
'Mother, come away', I plead.
I leave her waiting in the yard
or stirring at the range,
her large dark eyes,
her curling hair,
and wake to remember
what I have not done.

I have wished for her looks,
her bouncing wit,
her boundless, selfless love,
while I stood
in the no-woman's land
between two persons,
fighting the least lovely war with myself.
The family remember her excellence.
'Of course, she was a saint'.
And, wicked, I think how she laughed
and could have saved us.

Thirteen years dead
to patriarchy,
and they return to him,
forget the huge battles
she fought to keep the smile
that made us happy.
But I am breaking through the
silent walls.
She came to me at last,
a witch like me,

wrapped in power.
She spoke.

'You must travel
the unchartered path.
Your way is sin,
but so is the way of death.
There is no church here
to build a proxy world
and make us hate the real.
I have not lived so much as now'.

She spun to a black tornado cone,
came over me and, spinning,
entered all my skin.
She is here now,
in the world of my self,
moving with me towards a life.
I can begin
to forget the smiling frustrations,
the futile hope for heaven.
There is no holding
now I have cut loose
and she has come away.

The Disaffected Country Girl and A Minor Metropolis

A Minor Metropolis

She wanted to ride on the back of the world and here
was her creature.
No dung-shoed hooves or tangled fur, no hay-baked
breath.
She had read her Joyce and O'Brien, and latched.

Here she had food without oven smells. McDonalds
was Mecca
for cheapened protein; coins glugged in the tidal drive
of theatre, clubs, Indian skirts and beer.

She snuffled and picked up a whiff of direction. The
end of a corridor
shimmered ahead. Steel or water? Portal or foil?
Picking a thread on O'Connell Street, she followed the
clue.

Followed it badly, confounded by mazes internal,
stuttering
genes or history's hidden bombs. Held herself
bound by no rule or reason, untied to career
definition.

Here was the head in a stupor, making legends of
drunken romances,
giving credence where nothing was due, currying
virtue.
Believed herself god when spouting her parroted
wisdom.

And plans were made. And marriages. And better
jobs.

While she, trawling the streets for miracles,
became the consciousness zombie –
body moving, comprehension nil.

The Disaffected Country Girl

Life was elsewhere.
The to-other-views idyllic grass,
being so many meaningless spikes, and so present,
was ensconced as the meme of boredom.

She hoarded definitions.
So far, as with many in the same strangle of woods,
no compass had been proffered.
Enquiries had met with narrowed eyes.

Silence is not disapproval,
but the mother kept her distance from the main road
and the girl had a canine tendency to chew.
Puzzles were shelved, but fingers tested taboo pies.

God died. She drank on his grave,
her mother's too, and built a new philosophy.
Precepts grown in grass, oddly,
can be unyielding, like test-tubes.

THAT CONVENIENT BOYFRIEND

He was a something. That wasn't a farmer.
A photographer. Took her photograph.
She was round-faced. Podgy since Mammy died.
But he liked her. She never questioned that.
Might love her even. Whatever love was.

She saw his tongue too often.
It was over-active, like a swinging latch.
He had principles. Minded his mother.
Long-term plans. He'd marry a girl much younger.
She couldn't analyse. Too busy trying to kiss.

The Beloved

Thin as a poker. Something like de Valera,
but not cold. His voice milked her with its practice
in that large, opinionated, learned postman's family.
Tuned and sharp for the professor he would become.
He walked her home and said she always had a retort.
But she should move her hips when she danced.
He was the do of Latin verbs, the Stephen
in her Dedalian desires, the *Young Dog,*
the smile in her west moon.
'I love you', she told his long,
departing spine.

THE MAKING OF A CIVIL SERVANT

In country schools there are family legends.
'Your sister never lied'. 'Your grand-uncle
set up the town's branch of the Gaelic League'.
'Your mother is a lady'.
'Your father is a blow-in, an oddball'.

She was a quiet one. Lost in each sensate second.
And a volcano, throwing up without pre-rumble.
The class was a function of unreadable faces,
lives she couldn't lead. She drew no conclusions,
no lucky straws.

A star student, second only to the draper's daughter,
whose blond hair and pink skin went before her
like a pillar of light. To think that being human
and in this town could look scrubbed as that,
a polished glass.

The family name, she discovered, pointed to service.
Bó-ghiolla. Cowherd. But you needed brains
to work for the government. Brains, no cop.
Way to go when your intelligence was shy,
unfocused, boxed by schooling, romantic perhaps.

Or needing to be minded. Like hers. Lacking style
or genetic pass, no club would seek her out.
Nothing would have pleased her better than to swan
across a campus with chin arrogantly set,
but some wild things can't fight for position.

Failing a college grant her father had no plan,
she no resources. What followed was prison-break.
A steady income, such a paradox, is independence.

Signed herself into the institution. Circumscription
and official secrecy reduced to what they bought,
the drink, the animated talks, the extra-murals,
the undead hope of relevance.

In Herself

So far inside herself, and probably
(you might say) loving it,
she wanted to stay linked,
buttered to the first slice,
uneaten.

Though if eaten, better by mouse
than by man, whose teeth,
savage concepts, sharpen
on the forehead before chewing
the brain.

Then her field and her recondite room,
now the wainscots of her flat,
bred albino scuttlings,
pressed against the plastic-
packed air.

That is to say, she sat and heard
nothing but neural clicks,
had no name for them,
so listened all the more,
glued.

Domicile

Buried like this:
alive in grass. Domiciled in roots,
dark and light had been her round dance.
And what did she know of dance,
but an aborted section of a minuet
in fourth class? The typical half-measures
of her cracked cup.

Not bitter yet,
she found principles to uphold.
The flat was sub-standard, she knew,
but testing the limits of her remove,
she gave herself instructions to transcend.
Paupers find it noble to endure their lack,
de-wanting.

HER ODD WAYS

Eunan
Hardly ever smiles. A culchie,
but her talk is high-falutin.
Thinks she's the bees knees.
Probably reared in cotton wool,
the way she stays aloof.
Dresses all wrong, everything shapeless,
but I reckon there's a body under there.
Not a shred of interest in me, though.
I'd swear she saw me on the bus,
and the vacant seat.
Turned the opposite way.

Tom
Unusual. Sitting on her own.
I pretend the rest of the train is full.
Perfect colour combining. Smooth voice.
Total smile. When she smiles.
Knows how to wear accessories.
Other girls must envy you.
She doesn't understand.
Definitely middle-class. Idealistic.
Interested in self-improvement.
Extra-mural classes. Go-ahead.
She'll meet. Lucky me.

Hat and coat from *Wallis*.
Rare elegance.
Class company.
Ignore her discomfort in *Quo Vadis*.
The flat shocks me. Kip.
Couldn't do it here.

She's turned awkward.
Can hardly make a cup of coffee.

Spend a night in my place.
Steamy my eyeball.
With all the signals,
fainting eyes, unguarded talk,
I thought she'd have tricks,
at least wear a *baby-doll*.
But no.
Long t-shirt and a blank face.
No sex, not before marriage.
She can't be serious.
Said she wasn't religious.
She might have punched me.
I play the social worker.
Has a man ever come with you?
Yes. Pause. *How do you mean?*
Jesus! Total droop.
The legendary virgin.
Can't go there.
Too strange a frontier.
Another one bites the dust.
And how.

Ugly on the Inside

You think us expert in our various effects,
that this girl, pretty in the skin, knows her impact
exactly, how men quiver at the turn of her chin
and the strut of her hips, and how her
boatneck sweater makes them wonder if her
nipples are Bologna, Muffin Tops or Puffles.
You suppose she has planned her life according
to her beauty, grasping her desserts, just or other.

But eyes are outlookers. Behind, many points
of view collide. Bacteria make cogent arguments,
and germ cells, and somatic. Brain rules the
roost by several committees, more devolved
than any democratic state. Clamour always,
and the News alarmist. It takes a skilled cortex
to install a lovely avatar and steer the lot safely
to some harbour.

Mirrors, shout the gossips, *are never still,*
glass tending to flop.
The girl, dysmorphic, stares.

EATING OUT

food palace
no stain will settle on the cushioned plastic.
coffee could bog and you'd not be disordered.
disappeared only into another gap. fetch up
shining and sharp, whetsome for a raid,
no history.

you credit the legless consumers with pre-birth
hesitation. pins that have fallen from the hand
and will not be placed. the red nudges the blue
and they giggle the mirth of the forgotten.
you trick the eye with your deft rolls.

old men should be wanderers.
and young women.

she's surprised they ask her family name and origin.
she has not begun, don't they know, to call herself.
she is arty not artist, servant uncivil, urbane rustic,
universal irish, limerick by element only.
name her *alpha*.

the *aero* she eats, the éclair, will not keep her
in the gross dimension. she weights the pages of her
kafka with a cheap steel tray of condiments. she
will not be squared by desk and *opw* biro. a stranger
will arrive and find her new.

Fairview Café
Twelve, and Anne is noon incandescent. Glancing
up once, he has mapped her position. Closes
door and face and shuffles in, chuckles, slides to
sitting and menu.

'Haircut, Michael? Suits you'. She stands and coaxes
words to leave their terrified homes in deeply
strangling penitentiaries. 'Y-yes, Anne', he
stammers, 'A good job'.

Coffee happens, prettily ghosted by youthful
servers. All are acolytes. Doubling, Anne is
also Vesta, breath of the welcome fire and
bone of old principle.

Birds leave branches, rabbits their burrows, squirrels
hoarded treasures, just to be sunned in waves of
herness. Michael, tenant of darkened corners,
joins them in worship.

What makes myth in utilitarian eras?
What we know and take as a given? *Poor Town*,
woman sparing time for a reject. Reject
gentling his hungers.

Every Thursday, faithfully, myths are making,
walking, scribing strong in his childless psyche.
Only told by proudly remarking how, up in
Anne's place, they know him well.

Soul Kitchen, Swords
The baby sagely seems to understand,
for all his newness to the human scene,
that his father couldn't face the task
of cooking rashers on a Saturday,
when all week long a PC's saurian eye
has held him ageing in its tearless glare,
devising schemes to keep its clients happy.
Home has become a dreaded, tiring chore
that steals the music, reading, films, he'd prefer.

The baby, cheerful, bops a little to
the tong of a blues guitar, swings his legs
on the high and cosy chair, sets to chew
his toast as though it were the treat it is
to have a warm and pleasant breakfast.
His father never meets his eye, face
held stiff and straight, as though precarious.
Any minute now, it looks, this place
might show true colours, faithless as his life.

The baby positively contemplates
each random bit of information in
this virtual home, looks calmly as,
when wheeled inside, a peer sighs and grins,
resigned to his imprisoning harness.
The baby doesn't think to give his day
more meaning than the smell of milk and toast,
a smiling waitress, a colour parade,
a father, however zombie, a curious brain.

Unsatisfied Customer
There's an air about the woman that proclaims a lack
  of love.
The clothes are first to intimate.
Striped, loose-necked sweatshirt and a quilted gilet.
Nothing that suggests she might have shape.
Healthy though, as many de-loved women are.
Nunnish, everything planned, in place and regular.

Her eyes are dull stones cut in half by standard
  frames,
making every look a glare.
Thin, parched cheeks and incisive fingertips,
shoulders held as though by fiercer joints.

She looks like a worker, probably a bureaucrat,
for whose generation 'pensionable' meant 'intellect'.

She seems to think her presence has been purposely
 ignored
by the black-maned waitress.
Underlined marcasite eyes, firm-breasted, slim,
there's little doubt the girl's back is many-kissed.
If she sees the younger's born capacity for give,
it only shows in her rasp that it's been *six minutes*.

She orders fussily – a manor-lady or a fallen queen –
eats her dinner like a convent girl, neat bites,
perfect finger-hold, expert team of knife and fork.
Tutored, probably, in etiquette, in hope
that she would nab a doctor or a teacher, or at least
a higher civil servant, white collar pressed.

She looks nowhere, smiles at no new face, all intents
converged now on a measured day –
a meal, a walk by the sea, the *News*, the latest *Booker*.
That's not to say she's pulled a tragic card.
She's firmly here, in background noise and calculated
 chews,
maybe chuffed she's learned the secret to anonymous.

Anaerobic

There are still black skies in the spaces between towns.
He grew there like a night-flowering plant, petals
hard,
bent upon themselves, a long-lasting coat from a local
shop.

His parents fed him bread and closed subjects:
the price of things; who died how young; the means to
a living.
The city is a means, his surrogate vehicle, a lesser
wanderwomb.

The inexpensive, convenient flat is an exercise in
caving.
Negotiate the local *Leader* stained by grease and tea,
and there's the single bed, dully mined by a once-
washed coverlet.

There are women, now and then, in their less stagnant
pads,
but never one who doesn't baulk at how his moleish
head
sinks senseless, or tunnels, nothing pondered, to the
box.

He marries nonetheless, a po-faced woman from back
home.
In the same frame they buy a house in some functional
suburb,
begin there the long plod, the default mode to
oblivion.

SOLARIUM
Swords, Dublin

Thursday at seven in March and the sun sheening
pale yellow on the nondescript wall of *JC's*
supermarket.
Defiant boys swagger before cars, cursing the stranger.
There's a glare on the *Dunnes Stores* window, where
signs proclaim yet another sale, and women with high
hair
and low ear-rings clipclip through the doors like
proud minions.

How do we grow old here, in this trapping of sun, not
see
the total tragedy of sagging chins and folded-fan
faces?
Tell the ants to study this. No reluctance in the eyes
behind
trolleys, everyone a-focus, foraging among the tall
hills
of boxes and bottles, red, gold, blue, and greener than
grass.
Steering their own winding tracks amid the native
stream,

immigrants buy their meat and wine, stand out like
proud deer,
the only style in the mix. Why does the woman in the
beige coat
need four large cartons of *Flora* and a trolley tiered to
toppling?
Behind the check-out, the Latvian girl speaks her
language to two

compatriots. Being assistant manager is a cool coup for the man
in uniform, legs spread, every incomer a challenge.

You could almost believe there's meaning, though a small boy,
standing in a sun-slant outside the door, definitely scratches his anus.
His mother trundles distracted with two light-footed siblings,
grabs the busy hand and pulls him along. Home, no doubt,
will glow with this week's goodies. Mam, tired from shopping,
will slap up *Crispy Chicken* and chips and they'll watch a DVD,

the boy's thumb reminding him of all that's beneath appearance.
The city was always like this, the same brokered feel
on a March evening, sun sticky-fingered in the same way,
and me in the mix, doing what is done, because something
is churning. I allow myself to be victim to the offer
of cheap candles and discounted wine. Glister at least.

Across the road, a teenager off the bus from school
strolls home in his grey uniform, haloed by the setting light,
earphones firmly in.

Urban Eremitic

The dawn chorus is whirr of travel,
flap of received signal, urgent twitter.
I receive it in the throat of a fluent wind,
brave thing bearing a big worm.

These clanging frenzies are my company,
clamour of strivings in the spread hive.
Cells are piled upon cells, then space, then all
those far happenings, billions, without voice.

This is my nature, grown to steel and engine,
breathing in asphalt and granite, always stirred.
There never was silence. Below screech of aircraft,
gurgle of filling hot tank, hum of bathroom extractor,

there is the electric system within, the circulation
of the blood. I hanker out from this red brick umbrella,
but if birds weather it, can't I? Squirrels leap
in the minimal park, foxes streak across roads.

My feet spring off the virtual turf of a bicycle lane
as I walk in Rivervalley Estate, between green verges
and poker-faced houses. Suddenly cavil
in a tiny, stripped tree; for every absent leaf a bird,
garrulous as be-damned.

When I Was Ant

When I was ant, tick, beetle, low-scuttling to the
grains,
a blade of grass was sequoia, not green but seismicity,
but wind in the eyes, a bulge and a danger, thump of
foot
no lingoed thing, only world changing.

So I rode it, hid in its grooves, in the darkness large
as nosight, drop that is ocean, burred to its back,
its decoration, its untied button and its stamp.
Wheee, I cried, and nothing heard but the ant next
door.

Now I am tall as saplings, pushing out the
troposphere,
can straighten up and look, there's the real thing.
Climb no sequoias though, push down no oaks but
by tool. I am axe, knife, whisk and can opener, cyborg.

Then world sends light through my apartment
window,
lens of built box, incidental body, voile of dust and
drops
on the glass; once bright, twice askant. I am lamped,
waiting for the next move – dream, death or dry retch.

Yellow rises over scope of houses, grimalkin clouds in
its wake, while skin of the planned grass shivers from
meddling wind, naked trees wag and bow. Strike
peach and pink into the picture and the room changes,

makes me sequacious, shrinks me to a drop, burns me
to hydrogen and burns again. What am I? World
butters the sky, spreads on slices of lives, eats me

in this morning moment, when I am aardvark, rabbit,
badger, city cat, fish in a bowl, everything.

Green, Simply

Picture this: a girl in a green field.
There is no perspective. It's a flat scene she walks,
turned from you. Her face doesn't matter.
It's the back of her head that speaks.

She is etched on the screen inside,
slinking lankly out, colourless, feet and face
at odds, blindly reaching towards this new body.
Rehouse, avatar. Replicate me.

For all her walking she has no direction,
and the aspects of this green have no names.
The nearest would be: fingers, clumps, spatters,
tufts, sun speckles, grasshopper leaps.

She never even bends deep to see frogs.
It's enough to crouch like one of them,
feel the brush of the meadow on her thighs,
be an unquestioned eye of the sun's kindling.

Grows, yes, but the instrument stands while the note
is raised or bent. You will not hear her in the audience
when the titter is general; nor will her shoulders shake.
Still cell in the great unbrokered.

Lately she has seen a frog and recognised it
as a promise, its leaflike markings. She whispered,
Don't catch it. Don't box it. Don't let the dog smell.
Don't you know that all things, however embedded,
have a beat,
and hold to themselves,
greenly,
simply.

Home from Australia

My mother taught love by sacrifice, pitched on the low
altar of the lay,
torched by the tongues of marriage, charity and mystic
aspirations.
In the shadowed wake of the tyrant eye, she voiced
her other myth –
a hare, running impossibly through a man's outspread
legs, pole-vaulting
over the demesne gate. I hunted for myself in the
jungle of it.

Until my aunt came home, heralded for years by table-
cloths
leafy with koala bears and stamped by iconic
kangaroos.
The tiny spoons in parcels would barely hold a bite of
egg,
but pictures told legends of bliss and desertion in
Goondiwindi.

Tall, large-boned, she crossed the road with a great
loping sprint,
all coat flails and albatross. Played gaming machines
like a warrior,
marched through her sister's memory, indignant as an
activist,
and cast the straight question, 'Why did she put up
with it?'

Hers was the official sacrifice, the Life, crucibled in
such quaking
trials as hard labour on the convent floor. She was no
willow, didn't
bend easily, though laughter seemed to bring what

give was needed.
She carved her thinking, tuned her muscles to the
tasks of the righteous.

Here dwelled my genes, rampant and couchant, in this
untwinned pair.
There they grinned in that physical propulsion,
stirring me bewildered.
What good is a driver when nothing will stop the
vehicle,
like a mighty bird careering on a felt path, in sight or
not

of a destination? The world spins on, mostly
unknown,
until one day a reflection is cast on your head
and you learn the unexpected, a thread of the cloth
that made you.
I had to concede, the aunt's was hope of a happier
colour,
a blessing I might not always need to deserve.

THE ANGEL WOOS

The ex-priest left his school for a Kerry cottage,
thereby proving he could so love the world.
His mind, that might slay a man with one slicing blow,
would not be decommissioned but laid down
among the homesteads in an old, ambitious project.

Born to cottages herself, and expected to love small
  worlds
baked into faces that burst from the tart ground,
she played quiet and swiped at inarticulate heads of
  flowers.
Her intellect deschooled among the green tongues,
unlike her brother, who glugged on culture-whorls.

Genes, maybe, held her to the pre-conditioned;
  wizards
turning data into acts. She was something like her
  father,
masterless. What wouldn't he have given to belong to
  Ussher's
troop, have the wide sky to walk under and realise the
  error?
Instead of shoeless Limerick and a rare taste for
  Dickens.

The link between a ranting man and the heroes was
  foggy,
hard to see through the slammed door to a path
  beyond.
What was she to history but the subatomic text in a
  mote's eye?
Or was that it, at all? Shakespeare and Eliot grooved
  like pop,

all sound no sense. Life goes singalong – a neglected
study.

You imitate a cat sometimes, clawing back on time,
ask
why you did this, not that, why you wandered
clueless
when there was so much to achieve and by now you
could
be somebody. History's habit of repeating,
regurgitating,
knocks you flat, and you wake atop the same cliff,
hanging.

So, among the clay-faced, little one trying to be big,
she's still wandering. The ex-priest never did the
distance
of her father's early-to-bed, his labourer's hands
clutching
Tristram Shandy or writing to the *Herald* with a chess
move.
All thinking to be angels, in this singularly human
groove.

Picturesque Newcastle West

The returning exile finds a whiter path
and fronds waving at the borders.
It might be projection, of course;
memory is a favourite chocolate.
South Quay harbours no ship
– at one end you'd almost miss the river –
and there she walks, who never looked up,
unseeing the art deco furnishing shop,
stamp of the new decade.
Here's her little game –
she can't step on the cracks and she counts
the footfalls between.
Over the low wall, King Heron rules a shaded island,
stillest flower in the wind.
The doctor's house elves through the trees beyond –
he of the venous nose and bulbous stomach.
Thought he was funny, threading catgut
to stitch her upper lip.
No street defines the town.
It might have fallen to earth in a fingered whisper,
grown itself from riverish breath.
Now you know why RTÉ said *picturesque.*
Her town admired, imagine.
A pretty rural haven, a place to put a bow on.
Lanes' is closed,
but once it was the last stop on the homeward trek,
where she squandered money and teeth.
You have dreamt of them often since Frances died.
It matters, then,
that you were strung on the same thread.
The girl fears anyone with swish –
bankers, teachers, big men.
She is barricaded as a beetle, shifting as a cat,
raptured in her small things.

You love her at last.
She is only pre-political, a stage,
like any creature delved in a pocket of space.

It appears we all come back, with horsepower,
sweeping the scene for a selfsame mark.
You keep the engine running
in case a touch on the old ground will hold you there,
eyes down, counting your steps.
Where is it you're going when you drive on,
the picture scanned and stored,
her bowed head shrunken to a pixel,
and the show due for re-run, over and over?

Poems from *The Making of A Pagan* were published in the following anthologies: *The Virago Book of Wicked Verse,* ed. Jill Dawson (London: Virago, 1992); *I Wouldn't Thank you for a Valentine,* ed. Carol Ann Duffy (London: Viking/Penguin, 1992); *Ireland's Women: Writings Past and Present,* eds. Katie Donovan, A. Norman Jeffares and Brendan Kennelly (Dublin: Gill & MacMillan, 1994); *Hearsay: Performance Poems Plus,* ed. Paul Beasley (London: Bodley Head Children's Books, 1994); *Poems in My Earphone,* ed. John Agard (Harlow: Longman Literature, 1995); *The Field Day Anthology of Irish Writing: Volumes IV & V: Irish Women's Writing and Traditions,* eds. Angela Bourke *et al.* (Cork: Cork University Press, 2002). In German translation: *Irrlandt, Ireland, Irland,* ed. Jürgen Schneider (Berlin: Druckhaus Galrev, 1992); *Nautilus Literarischer Taschenkalender 1996,* ed. Jürgen Schneider (Hamburg: Nautilus, 1996).

Poems from *The Disaffected Country Girl and a Minor Metropolis* were originally published in the following publications: *Orbis* #155, Spring 2011; *About Place Journal* (aboutplacejournal.org); *The Stony Thursday Book,* No. 12, Autumn 2013.

About the Author

Máighréad Medbh has published five poetry collections and a CD. Described as 'a unique presence in the Irish poetry scene', she was one of the pioneers of performance poetry in Ireland in the 1990s, and continues to impress audiences with her unique style and approach to text. Her method is to source the physical motivation behind the thought, mining the body for its reactions to chosen themes. In recent years Máighréad has written two elaborate fantasies, one for children. A book of aphoristic reflections on the lone state, *Savage Solitude: reflections of a reluctant loner*, was published by Dedalus Press in 2013, and her novels are available as ebooks in several formats.

www.maighreadmedbh.ie

Máighréad's poetry collections are:
Twelve Beds for the Dreamer, Dublin: Arlen House, 2010.
When the Air Inhales You, Galway: Arlen House, 2008.
Split in *¡Divas!*, Galway: Arlen House, 2003.
Tenant, Cliffs of Moher: Salmon Publishing, 1999.
The Making of a Pagan, Belfast: Blackstaff Press, 1990.